CAN YOU FIND IT IN A
RAIN FOREST

Dee Phillips

GARETH**STEVENS**
GS PUBLISHING

A Member of the WRC Media Family of Companies

This North American edition first published in 2006 by
Gareth Stevens Publishing
A Member of the WRC Media Family of Companies
330 West Olive Street, Suite 100
Milwaukee, WI 53212 USA

ISBN 13: 978-0-8368-7454-9
ISBN 10: 0-8368-7454-4

Gareth Stevens series editor: Dorothy L. Gibbs
Gareth Stevens graphic designer: Charlie Dahl
Gareth Stevens art direction and cover design: Tammy West

Picture credits: (t=top, b=bottom, l=left, r=right, c=center)
FLPA: 2, 4-5, 7, 8-9c, 9tr, 10, 14, 17, 23.
Every effort has been made to trace the copyright holders for the pictures used in this book.
We apologize in advance for any unintentional omissions and would be pleased to insert the
appropriate acknowledgements in any subsequent edition.

Printed in China

1 2 3 4 5 6 7 8 9 10 09 08 07 06

Words that appear in the glossary are printed in
boldface type the first time they occur in the text.

Contents

A Rain Forest

There is so much to see in a rain forest, from birds flying through the **canopy** to fierce creatures **lurking** in the **undergrowth**.

What can you find in a rain forest?

Sloth

Toucan

Jaguar

Iguana

Tapir

Parrot

Monkey

Viper

Vines

Sloth

A sloth may be the laziest animal in the world. It moves very, very slowly and spends twenty hours a day sleeping in the rain forest's tall trees.

A sloth stays still for such a long time that green **algae** grows in its hair.

A sloth has three claws on each **limb**. It hooks them around branches to hold on tightly.

When a sloth is active, it moves at a speed of only about 7 feet (2 meters) a minute.

Toucan

Toucans spend most of their time high in the trees. They are one of easiest kinds of birds to identify because of their enormous **bills**. Toucans use their big bills to reach into trees and grab food.

Its bright yellow, black, and red **plumage** helps a toucan recognize other toucans and find a **mate**.

A toucan's bill, or beak, can measure up to 8 inches (20 centimeters) long!

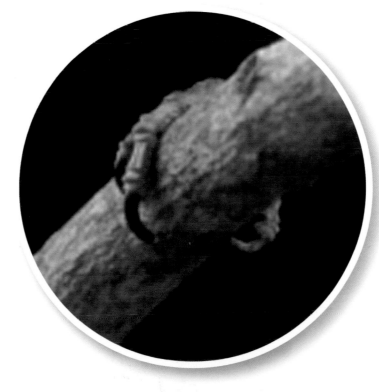

Toucans have strong feet that can wrap around branches to hold on tight.

Jaguar

Jaguars belong to the cat family. Most of these big cats have yellow coats spotted with black rings, but some jaguars are all black, and some jaguars are white.

The patterns on a jaguar's coat help it blend in with its surroundings. Each cat has slightly different markings.

Jaguars live in the wild in Central America, South America, and the southern United States.

A jaguar can swim very well and sometimes catches fish to eat.

Iguana

There are about 650 different kinds of iguanas. Some are very small, but the big ones grow to more than 6 feet (2 m) long.

The skin of a young iguana is very light green. This color helps it hide among the green leaves of the rain forest.

Iguanas are excellent climbers. Their long claws help them grip vines and tree branches.

An iguana spends a lot of time **basking** in the Sun to warm its body.

A tapir is an unusual-looking animal. It has a very large head, almost no neck, and its nose looks like a short trunk.

Because tapirs have such poor eyesight, they use their sense of smell to search for food.

When tapirs are frightened, they may dive into water to hide. They are very good swimmers.

Tapirs stay hidden from **predators** during the day. They come out at night to search for food.

A tapir has three toes on its back legs and four toes on its front legs.

Parrot

Parrots are noisy birds with bright plumage and powerful beaks. They live high in the branches of rain forest trees.

A parrot cleans its colorful feathers by carefully pulling them through its beak - one feather at a time.

A parrot has a hook at the end of its beak. It uses the hook to scoop out the soft parts of fruit. It uses its strong lower beak to crack open seeds.

Parrots have strong
wings and can fly
very fast over
short distances.

Monkey

Many different kinds of monkeys live in rain forests. Monkeys are part of the same family as apes and gorillas, but monkeys are smaller and have long tails.

The golden lion tamarin is a very small monkey – about the size of a squirrel. Its bushy golden mane makes it look like a lion.

Like most monkeys, tamarins spend a lot of time high in the trees, jumping or swinging from branch to branch. Their long, thin fingers help them hang on to the branches.

Most monkeys also use their long tails like an extra hand.

Tamarins spend all day in the trees, and at night, they even rest in the trees.

Viper

A viper is a **poisonous** snake. Its **fangs** fold up inside its mouth and swing downward when the snake wants to bite something.

The spiny scales over this viper's eyes look like eyelashes, The snake is called an eyelash viper.

A pit between a viper's eyes can sense differences in heat, which helps the snake find its **prey**.

Vipers in the rain forest usually rest during the day and come out at night to hunt. Their favorite foods include small **mammals**, lizards, frogs, and birds.

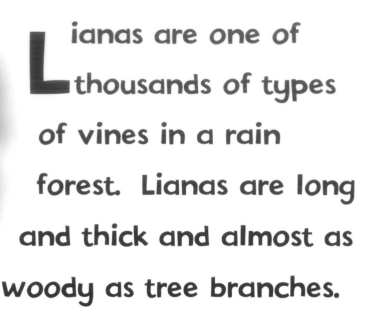

Lianas are one of thousands of types of vines in a rain forest. Lianas are long and thick and almost as woody as tree branches.

Most kinds of vines grow **tendrils**, which wind around trees to provide support.

Some types of vines are called strangler vines. They grow so thick that they can kill the trees supporting them.

As vines spread from one tree to another, they start to look like ropes draped across the rain forest canopy.

Glossary

algae – tiny plants that have no roots, stems, or leaves

basking – lying in the warmth of the Sun

bills – the mouthparts, or beaks, on birds

canopy – the highest treetops in a rain forest

fangs – hollow, pointed teeth used for biting and injecting poison

limb – an arm or a leg

lurking – waiting or hiding in a secret way

mammals – animals with backbones that give birth to live babies and feed their babies milk from the mother's body

mate – the male or female of a pair of animals that come together to produce young, or offspring

plumage – the feathers that cover a bird's body

poisonous – containing a substance that can cause illness or death

predators – animals that hunt and kill other animals for food

prey – an animal that is killed by another animal for food

tendrils – the long curls, or coils, of a plant that can grab on to or wind around something for support

undergrowth – the plants that grow under trees